To Ann Barr and
Gina and Murray Pollinger
P. B.

To Anna, Matthew,
and Jack
S. H.

and with thanks to
Michael Reynolds of the
World Parrot Trust
for his help and advice.

If you ever adopt a parrot, please MAKE SURE it isn't one that has been captured in the wild and imported. The international trade in wild birds is very cruel, and a bird that has been used to flying freely in a forest will never adjust to life with you. Make sure the parrot is one—like Turkey—that has been hatched and reared in captivity, in the country where you got it, and remember that you will have to devote a lot of time to its care, perhaps for the rest of your life.

Text copyright © 1994 by Penelope Bennett
Illustrations copyright © 1994 by Sue Heap

First U.S. edition 1995
First published in Great Britain in 1994
by Walker Books Ltd., London.

Library of Congress Cataloging-in-Publication Data

Bennett, Penelope.

Town parrot / by Penelope Bennett ;
illustrated by Sue Heap.—1st U.S. ed.

(Read and wonder books)
Originally published: 1994.
ISBN 1-56402-484-9
1. Blue-fronted Amazon parrot—Biography—Juvenile literature.
[1. Parrots.] I. Heap, Sue, 1954-   ill. II. Title. III.
Series: Read and wonder.
SF473.P3B455   1995
636.6'865—dc20   94–6409

10 9 8 7 6 5 4 3 2 1

Printed in Italy

TOWN PARROT

Penelope Bennett

illustrated by Sue Heap

CANDLEWICK PRESS
CAMBRIDGE, MASSACHUSETTS

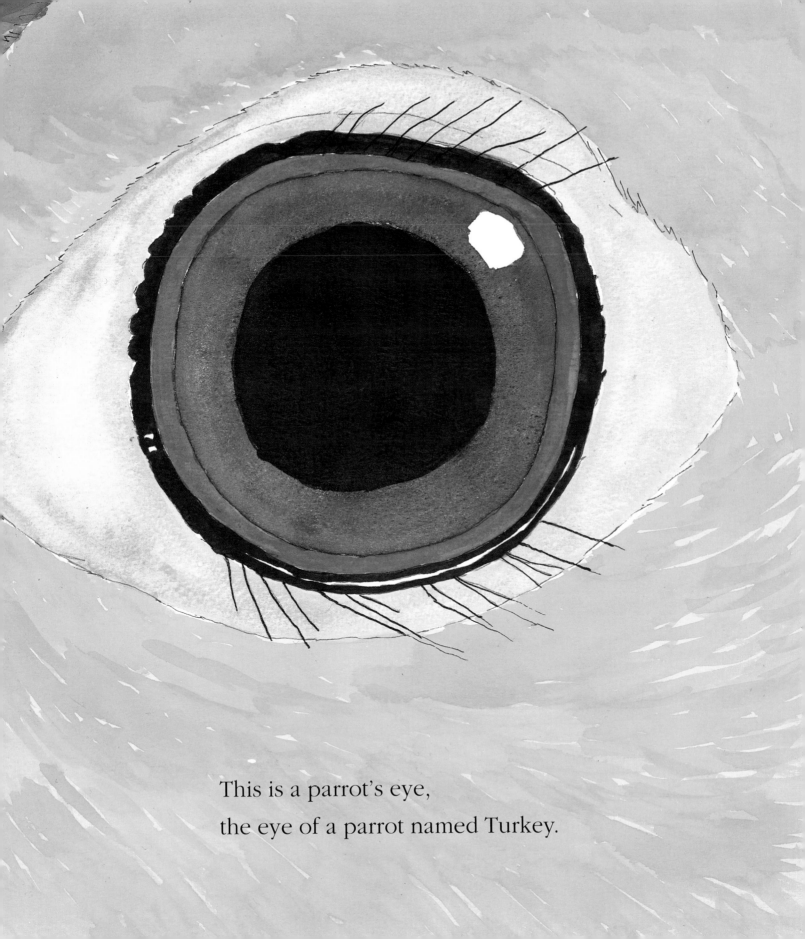

This is a parrot's eye,
the eye of a parrot named Turkey.

Turkey is a blue-fronted Amazon parrot. She looks as though she's flown through a rainbow.

The feathers on her head and body are small, soft, and rounded. Her tail and wing feathers are long and strong for flying.

She was hatched in an aviary,
six or seven years ago.

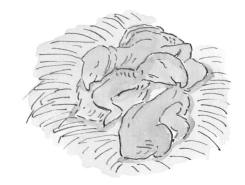

This is how she looked
when she was 7 days old . . .

15 days old . . .

26 days old . . .

6 months old . . .

Turkey could live
until she's 50 years old.

She should be living
in a tree in the
Amazon forest,
with a parrot family.
But she isn't.

She lives on the
top floor of a house
in town with a
writer named Ann.

Considering Ann's a human being,
Turkey gets along very well with her.

Ann works at home, so she spends a lot of time with Turkey. This is what parrots who live with people need.

Every day Turkey wakes up at about eight thirty and shouts, "Hello, Turkey!" in a rather hoarse voice.

While Ann takes a shower, Turkey grooms her feathers with her beak. Then she flies to the window and looks down at the people in the street below, whistling and calling to them.

A parrot's lower beak looks square from the front, like a chisel. The upper beak has ridges underneath, like a file. The tongue is strong, round, and black.

When Ann goes into the kitchen to make breakfast, Turkey rushes in too—her feet pit-pattering on the floorboards. She perches on Ann's shoulder and nibbles her ear.
If she's stirring oatmeal, Turkey waddles sideways down her arm and takes the spoon.

If she's eating granola, Turkey stands on her lap and picks out the nuts and raisins. When she finds a whole nut, she takes it between her toes and turns it around and around.

Parrots are the only birds who can feed themselves with their feet. With her feet, Turkey can waddle, climb, hold, cling, clasp, unpack, and pull.

After breakfast she has a snooze, her beak tucked into her feathers, her eyes half open, always alert.

As soon as she hears the mailman, she flies to the hall and watches the letters landing on the mat. Quite often she attacks them.

Parrots need to be busy. In the forest, they're flying, climbing, peeling bark, chattering, and cracking nuts. When they live with people who neglect them, they become sad, bored, and silent.

When Turkey wants to play,
she nips Ann on the hand.
If Ann's not in the room to
play with her, she likes
taking the spines off the
backs of books.

She also likes sorting
through cupboards and
drawers, tossing things out.
Her favorite cupboard
was the hat cupboard,
until Ann put the hats in
boxes. Now she likes the
kitchen cupboard best.

Sometimes Ann finds Turkey
hanging upside down in the hall.

When the telephone rings she attacks it. The last time the phone broke, the electrician said, "*Someone's* been messing with it." *Someone* sat swinging innocently on her perch.

Turkey has also removed the control knobs from several plastic clocks and uses them to play soccer.

Wires can be dangerous! People should be sure town parrots stay away from wires, out of danger.

Dear Tur
When
time

Turkey likes to eat vegetables, fruits, seeds, and nuts. For gnawing, she likes lilac, oak, and hazel bark.

Usually Ann and Turkey have lunch together.
Afterward Turkey takes a nap on Ann's bed.

Wild parrots nest in
hollow trees. Perhaps
under-the-bed feels
like a hollow.

Or she squeezes underneath it and talks
to herself in a strange little mewing voice.

In the afternoon she helps Ann with her window
box. She pulls out the sticks that Ann just put in.

Once a week Ann gives her a shower in the bathroom, then dries her gently with a hair drier. Turkey does her voice exercises in the bathroom, too, because that's the room where her voice sounds best. Ann used to think that she wanted her to listen, but she doesn't. She stops as soon as Ann comes into the room. But when *Ann* wants to listen to music, Turkey insists on joining in, piping and fluting. Sometimes they have whistling duets.

Parrots need showers. In the forest they rain-bathe in the treetops.

After dinner, Turkey watches
television. She likes the news, but
not the nature programs.

When sparrows come to Ann's bird table, Turkey
ignores them. But she never ignores cats or dogs,
however big they are. She tries to be friendly by
stretching out her foot to them.

When she stretches out her foot to Ann, it means that she wants to be picked up.

When Ann and Turkey go
away for the weekend,
Turkey travels free in the
baggage car, with the bicycles.

She also enjoys driving in
the car. She looks out the
window and purrs.

Ann sometimes takes her
to parties, where she's often
the most interesting guest.
When Ann dances, Turkey
sways backward and
forward on her shoulder,
screeching with pleasure.

When it's time to go to bed, Turkey follows Ann into the bathroom and watches her washing.

Then she wants to be taken to her cage and gets mad if she has to wait.

Once she's inside and her cage is covered, she's ready to go to sleep . . . until the next day arrives.